D0753549

RED WOLVES

by *Josh Gregory*

Children's Press®

An Imprint of Scholastic Inc.
New York   Toronto   London   Auckland   Sydney
Mexico City   New Delhi   Hong Kong
Danbury, Connecticut

Content Consultant
Dr. Stephen S. Ditchkoff
Professor of Wildlife Sciences
Auburn University
Auburn, Alabama

Photographs © 2014: Alamy Images: cover, 1, 12 (Brian Cook), 19
(M. Timothy O'Keefe), 4, 5 background, 16 (Mark Conlin), 5 top,
11 (Photo Network), 7 (Prisma Bildagentur AG); AP Images: 15
(Alan Marler), 23 (Bob Child), 39 (Phil Coale); Bob Italiano: 44
foreground, 45 foreground; Dreamstime/Kathleen Struckle: 2
background, 3 background, 44 background, 45 background;
National Geographic Stock/Joel Sartore: 5 bottom, 36; Superstock,
Inc.: 8, 20, 24, 27, 40 (Animals Animals), 28 (Biosphoto), 32 (Cusp),
2 inset, 3 inset, 31, 46 (FLPA); Visuals Unlimited/Jim Merli: 35.

Library of Congress Cataloging-in-Publication Data
Gregory, Josh.
 Red wolves / by Josh Gregory.
 pages cm. – (Nature's children)
 Includes bibliographical references and index.
 Audience: Ages 9–12.
 Audience: Grades 4–6.
 ISBN 978-0-531-21227–1 (library binding) –
 ISBN 978-0-531-25437–0 (pbk.)
 1. Red wolf–Juvenile literature. I. Title.
 QL737.C22G734 2014
 599.773–dc23   2013018346

Printed in China 62
SCHOLASTIC, CHILDREN'S PRESS, and associated logos are
trademarks and/or registered trademarks of Scholastic Inc.

1 2 3 4 5 6 7 8 9 10 R 23 22 21 20 19 18 17 16 15 14

Red Wolves

Class	Mammalia
Order	Carnivora
Family	Canidae
Genus	*Canis*
Species	*Canis rufus*
World distribution	Most live in zoos or breeding facilities; wild red wolves are found in refuges along the U.S. Atlantic and Gulf coasts
Habitat	Forests, wetlands
Distinctive physical characteristics	Reddish fur that can also include black, brown, gray, and yellow; males typically weigh 60 to 80 pounds (27 to 36 kilograms); females typically weigh 40 to 60 pounds (18 to 27 kg); around 26 inches (66 centimeters) tall at the shoulder; around 4.5 to 5.5 feet (1.4 to 1.7 meters) long, including the tail
Habits	Live in family groups known as packs; primarily active at dawn and dusk; avoid humans
Diet	Mainly eat meat, including deer, raccoons, rabbits, and rodents; occasionally eat berries and insects

RED WOLVES

Contents

CHAPTER 1

A Rare Breed

The sun disappears behind the trees on the horizon, and it begins to grow dark. A light breeze blows across the surface of a nearby pond, rustling the leaves of the plants along the water's edge. It is a warm spring evening in the wetlands of the Alligator River National Wildlife Refuge in North Carolina. The pleasant weather has drawn more people than usual to the refuge's hiking trails. Voices ring out as the hikers point out wildlife to one another and discuss the refuge's natural beauty. Meanwhile, a pack of red wolves lies quietly inside a hollowed-out tree. Only after all signs of the humans have disappeared will these rare and secretive creatures emerge from safety and begin the evening hunt.

The red wolf is seriously endangered. The species came close to extinction. This was mainly because of irresponsible human activity occurring up until the mid-20th century. Only in recent years has the red wolf begun to recover.

The endangered red wolf is a rare sight, even at the refuges where it is most common.

Home Sweet Home

Red wolves once lived throughout the eastern United States. They roamed along the coasts of the Atlantic Ocean and the Gulf of Mexico as far north as Massachusetts. They ranged inland to the Midwest, to states such as Illinois and Missouri. The wolves felt at home in swampy wetlands, dense forests, and even mountainous **habitats**.

Today, red wolves have disappeared from almost all of these places. Instead, they are found mostly at zoos and special **breeding** facilities. These organizations are scattered across the United States. The only wild red wolves living today are found in wildlife refuges such as Alligator River National Wildlife Refuge and Pocosin Lakes National Wildlife Refuge in North Carolina. These and similar refuges cover a few million acres of land. They are located near the coast in eastern North and South Carolina and northwestern Florida, and on Horn Island off the coast of Mississippi.

At zoos and breeding facilities, red wolves are fenced in to keep them safe from the dangers they would face in the wild.

Colorful Critters

The red wolf is named for the reddish fur that grows on parts of its body. This fur usually grows behind a red wolf's ears, on its **muzzle**, and on the back of its legs. The rest of the wolf's body is covered in fur that ranges from brown and yellow to black and gray.

Red wolves look a lot like certain types of **domestic** dogs. The wolves have pointed muzzles, long legs, and furry tails. Adult male red wolves usually weigh between 60 and 80 pounds (27 and 36 kilograms). Females are slightly smaller. They usually weigh around 40 to 60 pounds (18 to 27 kg). On average, a fully grown red wolf is about 26 inches (66 centimeters) tall at the shoulder. It can measure 4.5 to 5.5 feet (1.4 to 1.7 meters) long from its nose to the tip of its tail.

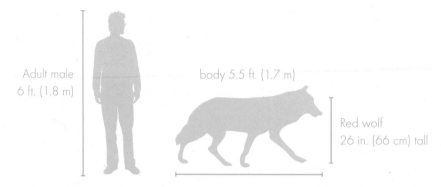

Adult male
6 ft. (1.8 m)

body 5.5 ft. (1.7 m)

Red wolf
26 in. (66 cm) tall

The fur around a red wolf's mouth is usually white or cream-colored.

CHAPTER 2

Powerful Predators

Red wolves are fierce carnivores. Though they have been known to eat berries and insects, their diet is made up almost entirely of meat. The average red wolf eats between 2 and 5 pounds (0.9 to 2.3 kg) of food every day. It is able to survive on many different kinds of prey, depending on what is available. However, because the red wolf is found over only a very small range, it does not have access to the same variety of food it once had.

Scientists have determined that white-tailed deer make up around half of a wild red wolf's diet today. Raccoons are another major source of food. They account for roughly one-third of an average red wolf's diet. Red wolves also hunt rabbits and a variety of rodents, including nutrias. A nutria is a large, water-dwelling animal that is similar to a muskrat.

Red wolves are among the most powerful hunters in their habitats.

On the Prowl

The red wolf is a highly skilled hunter. This predator has little to fear from the other wild animals it encounters. Each evening, a red wolf leaves its daytime hiding place to search for prey. Sometimes the wolf must travel a long distance before it finds something to eat. This takes time. As a result, these predators spend much of their time hunting. Red wolves are known to travel up to 20 miles (32 kilometers) per day in search of prey.

Red wolves do not often hunt in large packs. Instead, they most often hunt alone or in pairs. This is because much of their diet is made up of smaller animals. The white-tailed deer is the largest animal commonly hunted, and it can be caught without the help of a pack.

Red wolves change their hunting schedules during the winter. Instead of hunting at night, they are more likely to search for prey during daylight hours.

Red wolves stay on the move constantly as they hunt, traveling to a new part of their home range each day.

Built for Success

Red wolves locate prey using their remarkably sharp senses. Their sense of smell is the most important of all. A red wolf can catch the scent of prey from more than 1 mile (1.6 km) away. This sense of smell is more than 100 times as powerful as a human's is. Red wolves also have very strong hearing and vision.

Sometimes the red wolf directly smells its prey and begins chasing after it immediately. Other times, it must first track the scent trail left behind as the prey animal moves. Either way, the wolf relies on its powerful body once it locates its target. Red wolves are very fast runners, and as they move, their large toes can grip uneven surfaces. They are also strong swimmers, which enables them to follow prey across a variety of terrain.

Once the wolf reaches its meal, it bites down with its pointed front teeth. The top and bottom teeth lock together in a powerful grip that makes it difficult for prey to escape.

Red wolves sniff at the ground to follow the trail of potential prey.

CHAPTER 3

Part of the Pack

Red wolves are highly social animals. Though they often hunt alone, they live together in family groups known as packs. A pair known as the alpha male and alpha female leads the pack. The rest of the group is made up of this couple's offspring. Pack members can include recently born pups and young wolves born in previous years. The size of the pack depends on how much space the wolves have to roam and how much prey is available in the area. On average, red wolf packs are made up of five to eight family members. Sometimes a pack consists of only an alpha male and alpha female.

Pack members assist one another in many ways. They join one another on hunts and alert one another to food sources. They also help care for pups and fend off threats.

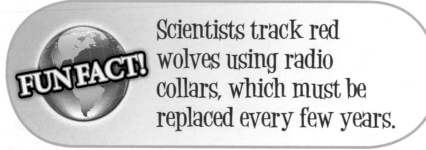

FUN FACT! Scientists track red wolves using radio collars, which must be replaced every few years.

Wolf pack members form close bonds with one another.

Mating Season

Red wolves **mate** once each year. Mating season usually occurs in the winter months, between January and March. The alpha male and alpha female are usually the only pack members to mate. The older offspring must leave the group and form their own packs when it comes time for them to produce pups of their own. Once red wolves choose their mates, the pair usually stays together for life.

Before a **litter** of pups is born, the parents must find a **den** where the mother can safely give birth. Red wolf dens are often in hollow trees or are holes dug into stream banks or hills. Other times, they are simply low areas surrounded by thick plant growth. Sometimes the dens are made from those left behind by other animals. Other times, the red wolf parents create the dens themselves.

FUN FACT! The Cherokee name for the red wolf is *wa'ya.*

A good den keeps a red wolf mother and her pups safe from harm when they are most vulnerable.

From Pups to Predators

Red wolf pups are born 60 to 63 days after their parents mate. Litters usually contain 2 to 8 pups, though they can occasionally include as many as 12.

Newborn red wolves weigh between 13 and 15 ounces (0.37 to 0.43 kg). Their eyes are closed, and they rely on their mother's milk for food. The pups are defenseless at first, so they stay hidden in the safety of the den. Once they are about six to nine weeks old, they begin eating meat that their parents bring to them.

As the young wolves grow stronger, they learn how to hunt and survive on their own. They become helpful pack members by the time their parents are ready to mate again the following year. When they are between two and three years old, they leave the pack and find mates of their own.

Many red wolf pups are born under the watchful eyes of wildlife experts.

Keep Out!

Red wolf packs live within areas of land called home ranges or territories. The size of a territory depends on how many wolves are in the pack and how much food is available in the area. Most territories are between 16,000 and 32,000 acres (6,475 to 12,950 hectares). Pack members defend their territory from other packs. They also fend off coyotes, which hunt many of the same prey animals as red wolves do. By keeping these rivals out of their territory, the pack ensures that it has plenty of food to hunt.

While red wolves are not afraid of most animals they encounter, they are not quite so fearless when it comes to humans. When they detect people within their territory, they run away and hide instead of attacking. In fact, there is not a single known example of a red wolf attacking a human.

FUN FACT! About 60 percent of the red wolf's recovery area in North Carolina is privately owned.

A red wolf's coloring helps it blend in with its environment and stay hidden from humans.

Staying in Touch

Communication is an important part of red wolf society. One of the main ways these animals share information is by howling. A red wolf's howl can mean several different things. It can be used to locate fellow pack members or discourage rival wolves from approaching. It can also be used to summon pack members to the location of freshly killed prey or to an area that needs to be defended.

Smell is another way red wolves communicate. Every red wolf produces a unique scent. As a wolf moves through an area, its body rubs against plants and other objects, leaving traces of this scent behind. Other red wolves can sniff these scents to determine where pack members and rivals have been and where they are going. A red wolf might follow a family member's scent trail to get from one hunting area to another. Unfamiliar scents might let a wolf know that there are enemies in the area.

Scents on the ground can help red wolves figure out where other wolves have traveled and in which direction they are heading.

CHAPTER 4

Canine Cousins

Red wolves are members of the Canidae family. Members of this family are often called canines or canids. Other canines include dogs, foxes, and jackals. Altogether, there are 34 different canine species. Canines can be found on every continent except Antarctica. These animals share many characteristics. For example, they are all predators, and most species are very intelligent. Most canines have long muzzles that contain 42 teeth. They also have long legs to help them chase after prey.

The earliest canines lived in North America around 35 million years ago. Over time, they spread into other parts of the world. These ancient canine species were similar to animals such as bears and weasels. The canines living today have not been around quite as long. For example, the domestic dogs that many people keep as pets first appeared around 12,000 years ago.

Some types of pet dogs look a lot like wolves.

Other Wolves

There are three different wolf species within the Canidae family. In addition to the red wolf, there are also the gray wolf and the Abyssinian wolf.

The gray wolf is by far the most common wolf species. It lives throughout North America, Asia, and northern Europe. Like the red wolf, the gray wolf is a top predator. No wild animal preys on it. Gray wolves look a lot like red wolves, but they are larger. An average adult male gray wolf weighs around 100 pounds (45 kg) and stands roughly 30 inches (76 cm) tall at the shoulder.

The Abyssinian wolf is also known as the Ethiopian wolf. It is the only wolf species found in Africa. Like the red wolf, it is an endangered species. Only a few hundred animals remain in the wild. Abyssinian wolves have reddish fur and slender bodies. Scientists once believed this species to be a type of jackal, rather than a wolf.

Abyssinian wolves are smaller than red wolves or gray wolves.

31

Close to Coyotes

One of the red wolf's closest canine relatives is the coyote. The two species look a lot alike and behave in similar ways. In fact, some experts believe that red wolves are the result of gray wolves and coyotes mating together years ago.

Adult coyotes generally weigh about one-half to two-thirds as much as fully grown red wolves. They also stand just a few inches shorter at the shoulder and have slimmer faces and bodies.

Coyotes were once limited to the plains of the western United States. Over the last 200 years, they have spread throughout North and Central America, including areas where wild red wolves are found. The two species compete for many of the same foods. However, unlike wolves, coyotes are not top predators. Powerful hunters such as cougars and even wolves sometimes kill them. Because they are smaller predators, coyotes are more likely than wolves to eat berries and other wild fruit when they have trouble finding prey.

Like red wolves, coyotes often fight each other to protect their territory.

CHAPTER 5

Struggling to Survive

Several factors led to the rapid disappearance of red wolves from the wild in the 20th century. For hundreds of years, the wolves were seen as threats to humans and livestock. During the late 18th century, authorities in parts of the newly formed and rapidly expanding United States paid bounties to people who killed wolves. Such attitudes only continued as the nation grew in size and population. Between 1932 and 1964, more than 50,000 red wolves were killed as a part of a predator control program created by the U.S. government.

In addition to intentionally killing the wolves, people also caused them harm by damaging their habitats. As the country's population grew and spread into new areas, natural environments were cleared away to make room for homes, businesses, roads, and farms. This left less space for red wolves and the animals they relied on for food.

Roads can be a major danger to red wolves and other wild animals.

RED
WOLF
CROSSINGS

NEXT
26 MILES

The Brink of Extinction

Red wolves came extremely close to disappearing forever. Experts believe that by 1970, there were fewer than 100 of the wolves left in the wild. These remaining wolves lived along the coast of the Gulf of Mexico in Texas and Louisiana.

In 1973, the U.S. government passed the Endangered Species Act. This law requires authorities to protect the country's endangered species from extinction. With its passage, scientists began working to save the red wolf. In the following years, they determined that only 17 of the remaining wolves were purebred. The rest were part coyote. The species had begun to die out in previous years, so the surviving wolves had trouble finding mates. They ended up mating with coyotes instead.

In 1975, U.S. authorities captured the 17 red wolves to begin a captive breeding program. With these wolves in captivity, the red wolf was officially declared extinct in the wild in 1980.

Wildlife experts use specially padded traps so that wild red wolves will not be hurt when they are captured.

A Slow Recovery

Of the 17 red wolves taken from the wild, 14 were chosen to begin rebuilding the species' population. The U.S. Fish and Wildlife Service sent the wolves to Point Defiance Zoo & Aquarium in Tacoma, Washington. There, experts cared for the wolves and made sure their pups grew up to be strong and healthy. Slowly, the red wolf population began to increase again. The new pups were sent to other zoos around the country, and today there are around 40 different locations where red wolves are bred in captivity.

In 1987, the U.S. Fish and Wildlife Service began releasing some of the captive-bred wolves back into the wild at Alligator River National Wildlife Refuge in North Carolina. Four mated pairs were released, and these wolves' first wild pups were born the following year. Under the protection of the refuge, the wild red wolf population has continued to grow. Today, there are between 100 and 120 wolves living in the wild. Another 200 or so now live in captivity.

Breeding programs release red wolves into refuges with tracking devices so they can record the wolves' movements in the wild.

What Comes Next?

Though captive breeding programs have been successful so far, red wolves are a long way from making a complete recovery. Authorities must work hard to ensure the species' continued survival. One major issue is that red wolves sometimes still interbreed with coyotes. This could result in fewer purebred wolves, just as it did before the breeding program began. The wild wolves are carefully monitored, and workers attempt to keep coyotes away from the wolves' territories.

Zoos, government organizations, and **conservation** groups work to educate the public about the difficulties facing red wolves. Many zoos offer information about the wolves. Visitors to the Alligator River National Wildlife Refuge can attend Howling Safaris, where guides teach them about the wolves and show people how to howl so that wolves will respond.

Red wolves face a difficult recovery, but their future is bright. With a little help, these amazing predators could one day roam throughout the country just as they once did.

With a little help, wild red wolves may one day roam as widely as they did in the past.

Words to Know

bounties (BOUN-teez) — rewards offered for the capture of a criminal or a harmful animal

breeding (BREE-ding) — mating and giving birth to young

captive (KAP-tiv) — confined to a place and not able to escape

carnivores (KAHR-nuh-vorz) — animals that eat meat

conservation (kahn-sur-VAY-shuhn) — the protection of valuable things, especially forests, wildlife, natural resources, or artistic or historic objects

den (DEN) — the home of a wild animal

domestic (duh-MES-tik) — tame; people use domestic animals as a source of food or as work animals, or keep them as pets

endangered (en-DAYN-jured) — at risk of becoming extinct, usually because of human activity

extinction (ik-STINGK-shuhn) — complete disappearance of a species from a certain area or from the entire world

family (FAM-uh-lee) — a group of living things that are related to each other

habitats (HAB-uh-tats) — places where an animal or a plant naturally lives

litter (LIT-ur) — a group of baby animals that are born at the same time to the same mother

livestock (LIVE-stahk) — animals that are kept or raised on a farm or ranch

mate (MAYT) — to join together to produce babies

muzzle (MUHZ-uhl) — an animal's nose and mouth

pack (PAK) — a group of related wolves

predator (PRED-uh-tur) — an animal that lives by hunting other animals for food

prey (PRAY) — an animal that is hunted by another animal for food

purebred (PYOOR-bred) — having ancestors of the same breed or kind of animal

refuge (REF-yooj) — a place that provides protection or shelter

species (SPEE-sheez) — one of the groups into which animals and plants of the same genus are divided; members of the same species can mate and have offspring

Habitat Map

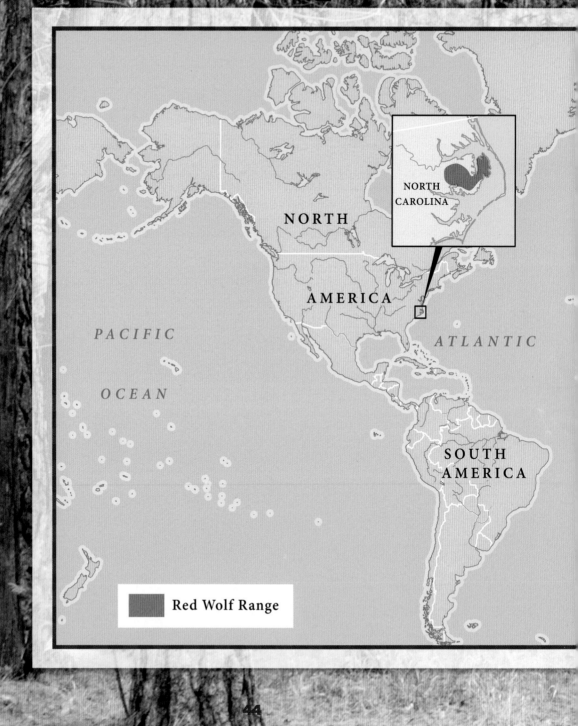

NORTH

AMERICA

NORTH
CAROLINA

PACIFIC

OCEAN

ATLANTIC

SOUTH
AMERICA

Red Wolf Range

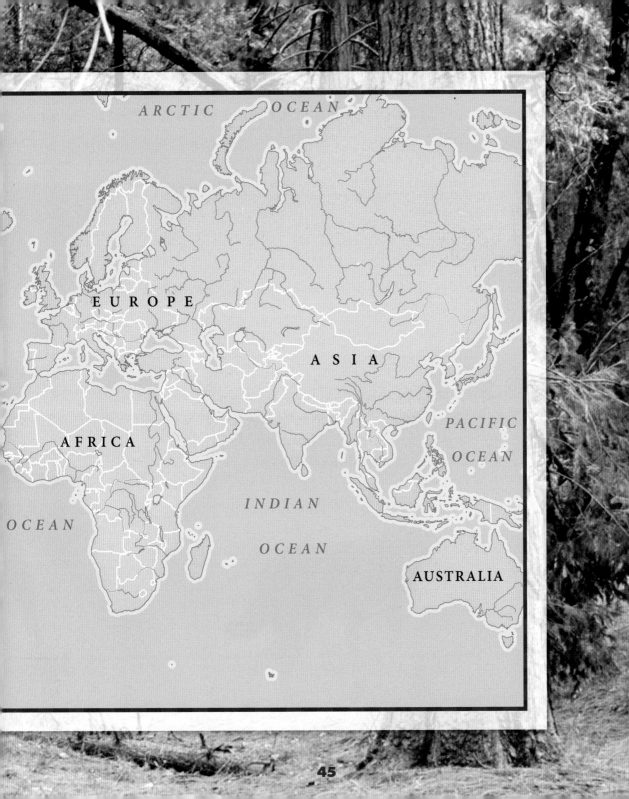

Find Out More

Books

Brandenburg, Jim, and Judy Brandenburg. *Face to Face with Wolves*. Washington, DC: National Geographic, 2008.

Goldish, Meish. *Red Wolves: And Then There Were (Almost) None*. New York: Bearport Publishing, 2009.

Imbriaco, Alison. *The Red Wolf: Help Save This Endangered Species!* Berkeley Heights, NJ: MyReportLinks.com Books, 2008.

Visit this Scholastic Web site for more information on red wolves:
www.factsfornow.scholastic.com
Enter the keywords **Red Wolves**

Index

Page numbers in *italics* indicate a photograph or map.

About the Author

Josh Gregory writes and edits books for kids. He lives in Chicago, Illinois.

Hanukkah

Publishing Company

A Buddy Book
by
Julie Murray

Visit us at
www.abdopub.com

Published by Buddy Books, an imprint of ABDO Publishing Company, 4940 Viking Drive, Suite 622, Edina, Minnesota 55435. Copyright © 2003 by Abdo Consulting Group, Inc. International copyrights reserved in all countries. No part of this book may be reproduced in any form without written permission from the publisher.

Printed in the United States.

Edited by: Christy DeVillier
Contributing Editors: Matt Ray, Michael P. Goecke
Graphic Design: Denise Esner
Image Research: Deborah Coldiron
Cover Photograph: Photodisc
Interior Photographs: Comstock, Corbis, North Wind Picture Archives, Picturequest, Photodisc

Library of Congress Cataloging-in-Publication Data

Murray, Julie, 1969-
    Hanukkah/Julie Murray.
        p. cm. — (Holidays. Set 1)
    Contents: What is Hanukkah? — Antiochus IV — The Maccabees— The first Hanukkah
— Hanukkah through the years — the menorah — Dreidels — Hanukkah food — Gift giving.
    ISBN 1-57765-953-8
        1. Hanukkah—Juvenile literature. [1. Hanukkah. 2. Holidays.] I. Title.

BM695.H3 M87 2003
296.4'35—dc21

                                                            2002026099

Table of Contents

What Is Hanukkah?

Hanukkah is a Jewish **holiday**. It is sometimes called the Festival of Lights. People often celebrate Hanukkah with stories, games, special foods, and gifts.

Hanukkah honors an important time in Jewish history. People celebrate Hanukkah in November or December. This holiday lasts for eight days.

Many Jewish people celebrate Hanukkah every year.

A Living Language

Hanukkah is a Hebrew word that means **dedication**. Hebrew is a very old language. It has been around for thousands of years.

The oldest Jewish writings are in Hebrew.

Today, millions of people speak Hebrew in Israel. This makes Hebrew one of the oldest living languages.

The Hanukkah Story

Hanukkah began more than 2,000 years ago. Back then, Jewish people lived in Judea. They were often called Judeans or Jews. The Jews prayed to one God. Their Temple was in the city of Jerusalem.

The Star of David is a symbol of the Jewish religion.

At one time, the Syrians ruled the Jews. One Syrian king was Antiochus IV. Antiochus IV ordered the Jews to give up their religion. He commanded them to pray to the Greek gods.

One day, Syrian soldiers went to the village of Modi'in. They ordered the Jews to kill a pig for the Greek gods. A Jewish leader refused. His name was Mattathias.

Antiochus was a Syrian king.

Mattathias gathered an army to fight the Syrians. He put his son Judah in charge of the Jewish army. People began calling Judah's skilled army the Maccabees. *Maccabee* is a Hebrew word meaning hammer. The Maccabees won and lost many battles. One day, they took back Jerusalem.

The First Hanukkah

The Syrians had destroyed much of the Temple of Jerusalem. So, the Jews rebuilt it. They took down the Syrian's statues of Greek gods. Then, they held a celebration to **re-dedicate** their Temple to God. They celebrated winning back their **religious freedom**. This is called the first Hanukkah.

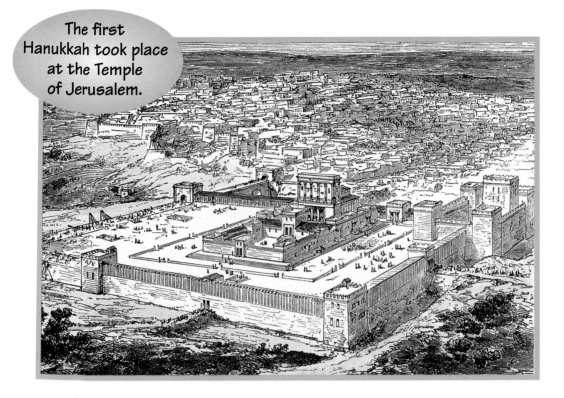

The first Hanukkah took place at the Temple of Jerusalem.

The Jews lit a **menorah** for the first Hanukkah. This menorah needed lamp oil to stay lit. The Jews believed there was enough oil for one day. But the menorah stayed lit for eight days. The Jewish people called this a great **miracle**.

A hanukkiah holds eight candles and the shammash.

The Jews did not want to forget the **miracle** of the **menorah**. Eight became a special number for Hanukkah. This is why Hanukkah is an eight-day celebration.

The Menorah

A special **menorah** used for Hanukkah is called a *hanukkiah*. These menorahs hold nine candles. The ninth candle is called the *shammash* candle. People use the *shammash* to light the other eight candles. The eight candles stand for the first Hanukkah menorah that burned for eight days.

The shammash sits higher than the other eight candles.

Lighting the *hanukkiah* is a **custom** of Hanukkah. This happens each night after sunset. One candle is lit on the first night of Hanukkah. On the second night, someone lights two candles. By the last night of Hanukkah, all of the candles are lit.

A Hanukkah Game

Games are part of many Hanukkah celebrations. One game uses a dreidel. A dreidel is a four-sided top. Each side has a Hebrew letter. The letters stand for four Hebrew words. Together, the words mean "A great **miracle** happened there." This reminds players of the miracle at the first Hanukkah.

Hanukkah Foods

Big meals are common at Hanukkah celebrations. Eating latkes is one Hanukkah **custom**. Latkes are also called potato pancakes. They are fried in oil. Foods fried in oil remind people of the **miracle** at the first Hanukkah.

Many people eat challah bread on the Friday night of Hanukkah.

Cheese reminds Jewish people of a famous story. This story is about a brave woman named Judith. She lived in the city of Bethulia. Judith had a plan to save her city from the Syrians.

One day, Judith brought a Syrian general some cheese and wine. After the meal, he fell asleep. Then, Judith killed him. This saved the Jewish people from a Syrian attack.

Another Hanukkah food is *sufganiyots*. They are jelly-filled doughnuts. Cookies in the shape of dreidels or stars are common, too.

Making Latkes

Ask an adult to help you make latkes. You will need:

2 medium potatoes

1/2 cup chopped onion

1 egg, beaten

1/4 cup flour

1/2 teaspoon salt

pepper (pinch)

vegetable oil

apple sauce or sour cream

1. Wash, peel, and grate the potatoes.
2. Press grated potatoes and onions in a colander to remove extra liquid. Then, put potato mixture into a large bowl.
3. Mix a beaten egg, flour, salt, and pepper into the potato mixture.
4. Heat vegetable oil in a large frying pan. Add spoonfuls of the potato batter. Fry both sides until latkes are golden brown. Serve warm with applesauce or sour cream.

Hanukkah Today

Today, giving gifts is common during Hanukkah. Some families give gifts each night. Other families give one gift each Hanukkah.

Long ago, people gave children coins during Hanukkah. This **custom** started long ago when the Jews ruled themselves. They began making their own coins, or gelt. Gelt is money. Today, children often receive gifts of chocolate money coins.

Some families
give children gelt
during Hanukkah.

Some families enjoy helping others during Hanukkah. They collect food and money for the poor. They put money in a *tzedakah* box. *Tzedakah* means justice.

During Hanukkah, people visit their **synagogues**. They sing songs and listen to stories. They think about what it means to have **religious freedom**.

Special events for Hanukkah take place at synagogues around the world.

Important Words

custom a practice that has been around a long time. It is a custom to eat latkes for Hanukkah.

dedication the act of devoting something to someone holy. The Jews dedicated the Temple of Jerusalem to God.

holiday a special time for celebration.

menorah a candleholder.

miracle something that goes against the laws of nature. Some people believe miracles are acts of God (or gods).

religious freedom the freedom to pray and worship as one chooses.

synagogue a special place where Jewish people gather to pray.

Web Sites

To learn more about Hanukkah,

visit ABDO Publishing Company on the World Wide Web. Web site links about Hanukkah are featured on our Book Links page. These links are routinely monitored and updated to provide the most current information available.

www.abdopub.com

Index